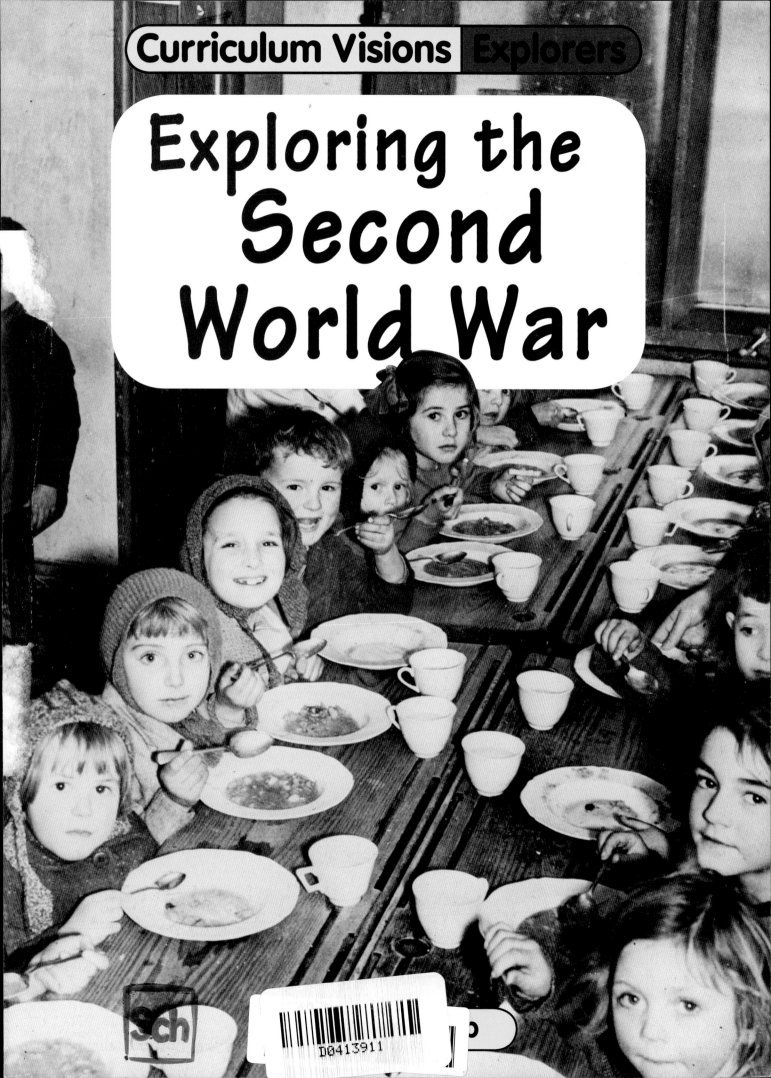

Exploring the Second World War

The Second World War was a terrible war that lasted for 6 years. Millions of soldiers, sailors, airmen and ordinary people were killed.

After the war, people did not want to forget these people and so they built crosses and put up plaques in their memory. These are called memorials. You will find memorials all over Britain, the Commonwealth and other places.

Each year the nation remembers these people (and those of other wars, earlier and more recent) and vows it will try not to let such dreadful events happen again.

ALSO IN GRATEFUL MEMORY OF THESE OUR BROTHERS
WHO FELL IN THE WAR OF 1939 - 1945

ERNEST F ANDREWS   FREDERICK C HOWARD   THOMAS R RICHARDS
PETER F BEARD   PERCY JACKMAN   ANTONY P TOMKINSON
JOHN M BLANDY   ALFRED R JENKINS   ERIC TUBB
LAWRENCE C CRANE   CECIL R DEE   WILLIAM J WALTERS
   MARTIN   WILLIAM WARD
   O PHILLIPS   ROBERT A WEBSTER

Second World War timeline

1938	1939	1940	1941
	3 Sept: War with Germany begins	Bacon, butter and sugar rationed	Dec 1941: USA enters the war
	Meat rationing begins	Home Guard created	
		Battle of Britain begins	

Gas masks issued   Evacuation of children begins   **The Phoney War**   Winston Churchill becomes Prime Minister   Blitz begins   Blitz ends in failure for Germany

Second World War (1939–1945)

| 0 | 1000 AD | 2000 AD |

00–146BC)

Anglo-Saxons (450–1066)

Tudors (1485–1603)

Victorians (1837–1901)

Romans (700BC–476AD)

Vikings (800–1066/1400)

"This morning the British Ambassador in Berlin handed the German government a final note stating that unless we heard from them by 11 o'clock, that they were prepared at once to withdraw their troops from Poland, a state of war would exist between us. I have to tell you now that no such undertaking has been received and that consequently this country is at war with Germany."

Neville Chamberlain,
Prime Minister, 3 September 1939

Contents

Look up the **bold** words in the glossary on page 32 of this book.

Britain begins to win the war in North Africa

Allied troops invade Italy

Germany fires the first rocket bombs at Britain

Hitler commits suicide

Some rationing stops

| 1943 | 1944 | 1945 | 1946 |

Allied invasion of France from Britain (called D-Day)

VE-Day to mark the end of war in Europe

Rationing not over until 1954

Meet the war-time children

Children do not start wars, but they do get caught up in them. Their dads may have to join the army, navy or airforce and they may not see them for years. In some cases their dads never came back from the war.

Mums had to work all day to help the war effort, so children were looked after by neighbours.

There was always the chance that their house might get bombed.

Things became scarce, and many items were rationed. So wartime children had to learn to make do with what was around.

Imagine your school being bombed! What would it feel like? These children were asked to make drawings of the recent bomb damage to their school. It was all the art teacher could do so soon after the bombing.

Did you know... ?

- Many children helped to grow food.
- Wartime children still had to go to school.
- Children wore school uniforms, even in the war.
- When clothes started to wear out they were **darned** to make them last longer.

Q What happened when children's clothes began to wear out?

In the years leading up to the war, children learned about **democracy** versus Hitlerism.

What was the Second World War?

No wars start for simple reasons. Usually they start because things have been going wrong for a long time. The bitterness that led to the Second World War began about ten years earlier in Germany.

Did you know...?

- That the Second World War lasted from 1939 to 1945.
- That about 20 million Russians and 4 million Jews were killed in the war.
- Germany had the support of countries like Italy and Japan. Britain had colonies all over the world. So when Britain and Germany went to war this immediately meant that war happened all over the world.
- Wars have happened in every century since records began.
- There are still people alive who can tell you what it was like for them.

The Germans are a proud people, but they had lost the First World War and in the early 1930s they were poor. They thought other countries were being unfair and they wanted a better life.

A small group of people, the Nazi Party led by Adolf Hitler, told the German people that they could make the Germans proud again. They told them that they would get back the lost German lands. Hitler told them they would have more food and more money.

Most people were so pleased to have a better life, they did not notice that their country was being taken over by people who would kill to get their way.

The dark side was truly horrible, with Jews, gypsies and many other people put in **concentration camps** and killed. Yet, somehow the German people did wake up to this.

Q **Who was the leader of the Nazi Party in Germany?**

Britain prepares for war

Hitler was a very bold and clever planner. He thought up a whole new kind of warfare using fast-moving tanks and bomb-carrying planes. The Germans planned to **conquer** western Europe in just a few weeks.

Once Hitler was ready, the German forces started to **invade** Germany's neighbours. At first, powerful countries like Britain and America did nothing to stop him. Britain had only just started to make new planes and weapons. It needed more time. But Britain had promised to help Poland if it were invaded. So, when Germany invaded Poland on September 3rd 1939, Britain was forced to go to war with Germany.

Did you know... ?

- The Second World War was the first war fought using tanks and aircraft.
- The Germans thought they could win their war in weeks, so they called it the Lightning War, which in German is *Blitzkrieg* (pronounced *blitskreeg*).

Britain prepared for the attack they knew would come. Barbed wire surrounds this airfield where precious Spitfires and Hurricane fighter planes wait to take off at a moment's notice.

	Britain and its allies
	Germany and its allies
	Defeated countries
	Neutral countries

The German *Blitzkrieg* plan was a good one. By the middle of 1940 most countries in Europe were defeated, leaving Britain to stand alone against the might of Hitler's Germany.

Q Why did Britain go to war?

The Battle of Britain

Germany's *Blitzkrieg* plan using tanks could not work with Britain, because to conquer Britain, Hitler had to invade by sea.

Hitler needed to get troops across the English Channel, and he could not do this if British fighter planes were still in the air. So his plan was first to destroy the British air force and its planes.

In July 1940 the Germans began bombing airfields, aircraft factories and early-warning (radar) stations.

The RAF commanders sent up fighter planes to attack them. With skill and determination they were able to shoot down large numbers of German planes. Because this air war was make or break for Britain, this time was known as the Battle of Britain.

Q Why was the air war called the Battle of Britain?

German Heinkel bombers over southern England.

Did you know... ?

- This was when the Prime Minister, Winston Churchill, made his famous speech in which he praised the RAF: "*Never in the field of human conflict was so much owed by so many to so few.*" It was nothing short of the truth.
- The German air force was called the *Luftwaffe* (meaning 'air weapon' and pronounced *looftwaffer*).
- The British had to destroy at least 4 German planes for every British plane the Germans destroyed, because the Germans had 2,400 planes and the British only had 640.
- Some of the most famous planes ever built were used in the Second World War: the Spitfire and the Hurricane fighters, and the Lancaster and Wellington bombers.

The British were ready to defend the shores using big guns that could destroy ships. They were placed all along the coast.

The Blitz

Hitler's bombing of airfields was very effective, but on August 24th 1940 a lost German bomber crew accidentally bombed London instead of airfields. Prime Minister Winston Churchill was shocked by this and he told the RAF to bomb Berlin, the capital of Germany.

Hitler was furious at this attack on his homeland. In a rage, he ordered the German air force to stop attacking airfields and to attack ports and cities instead. He thought that bombing the people would make them want to ask for peace.

The bombing of cities was the start of the time called the Blitz. The Blitz affected nearly all major cities, such as Glasgow and Liverpool, Coventry and Plymouth. From September 2nd 1940 London was attacked each night for 57 nights. Over a million bombs were dropped.

Although bombs were aimed at docks, factories and railway lines, many bombs fell on the surrounding streets and houses.

Did you know... ?

- Over 41,000 civilians were killed during the Blitz.

"If they send over a hundred bombers to bomb our cities, then we shall send a thousand planes to bomb theirs. And if they think that they can destroy our cities, then we shall wipe theirs from the face of the Earth."

Adolf Hitler
When the British bombed Berlin

"We shall defend our Island, whatever the cost may be, we shall fight on the beaches, we shall fight on the landing grounds, we shall fight in the fields and in the streets, we shall fight in the hills; we shall never surrender..."

Winston Churchill
When Hitler bombed Britain

A house after a German bombing raid.

Q **Why did Hitler decide to bomb British cities?**

Did you know… ?

- A special wireless detecting system called RADAR could pick up enemy aircraft as they started across the Channel. Air-raid **sirens** were sounded to give people time to take cover.
- At night people had to cover up all lights so that enemy planes could not spot cities from the air. It was called '**blackout**'.
- By mid October 1940 there were approximately 250,000 people homeless due to the Blitz in London alone, so there was a serious problem in finding shelter for them.

Being in an air raid

Imagine seeing the first wave of German planes arriving over London. It was four o'clock on the 7th September 1940. There were 340 bombers protected by 600 fighters.

Their target was the docks of London and their purpose was to drop fire bombs and set the docks ablaze.

There were so many planes that it was two hours before the planes had dropped their bombs and left for Europe.

The raging fires made a beacon of light for the night bombers, who didn't stop until 4.30 in the morning. Then the all-clear siren was sounded.

For nine months there was hardly a night when the air-raid sirens did not wail. Every night there was the whine of bombs and the bang of explosions.

But bombing Britain failed. Britain did not surrender. So, on the 10th May 1941, Hitler stopped the mass raids.

Houses on fire during the Blitz.

Q **What is an air-raid siren?**

How people protected themselves

The two big threats were from bombs and from poison gas.

In the First World War many soldiers had been killed and injured by poison gas released over the battlefields. So even before the Second World War started, the government gave everyone a gas mask which they had to carry at all times. As it turned out, gas was never used.

To protect against bombs, the government allowed underground railway stations to be used as shelters. Long trenches were dug in parks and roofed with bricks. At the start of an air raid people took cover in the trenches or underground railway stations.

This is the gas mask and helmet kit for an air-raid warden. Wardens had to patrol the streets during an air raid. The helmet is made from steel.

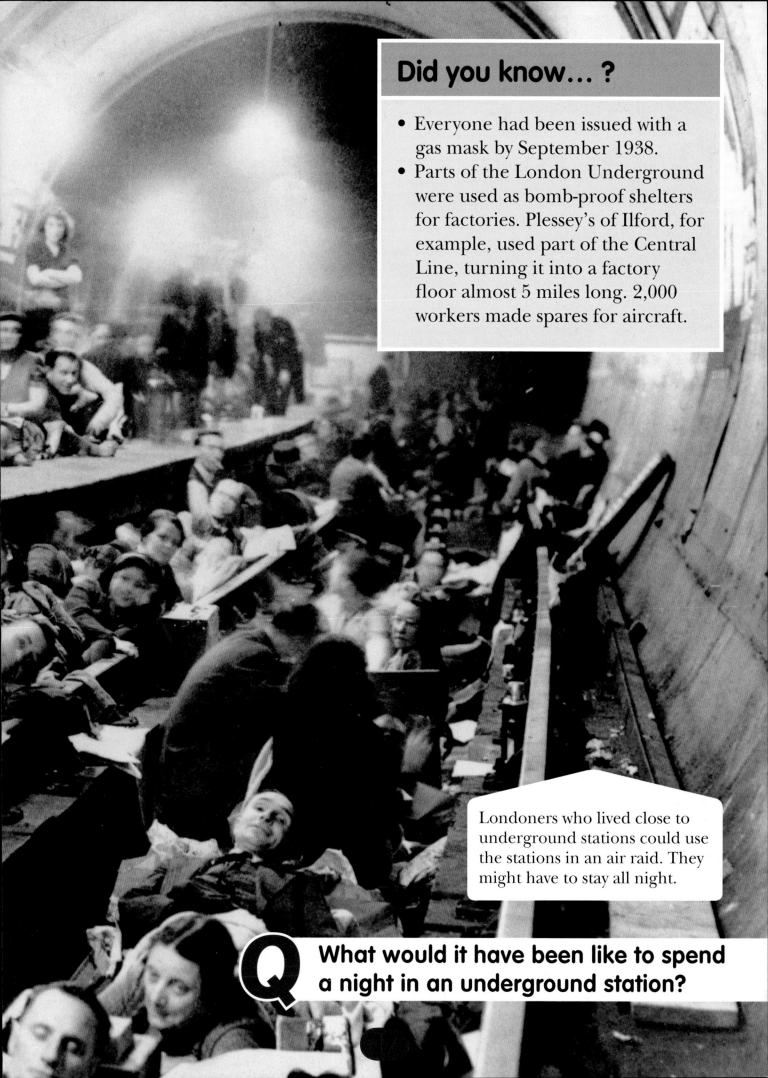

Did you know... ?

- Everyone had been issued with a gas mask by September 1938.
- Parts of the London Underground were used as bomb-proof shelters for factories. Plessey's of Ilford, for example, used part of the Central Line, turning it into a factory floor almost 5 miles long. 2,000 workers made spares for aircraft.

Londoners who lived close to underground stations could use the stations in an air raid. They might have to stay all night.

Q What would it have been like to spend a night in an underground station?

Sheltering at home

It could be a long way to a government shelter. So, many people decided to take their chances at home, perhaps in a small shelter in the garden, perhaps in a cellar, perhaps sleeping under the dining room table.

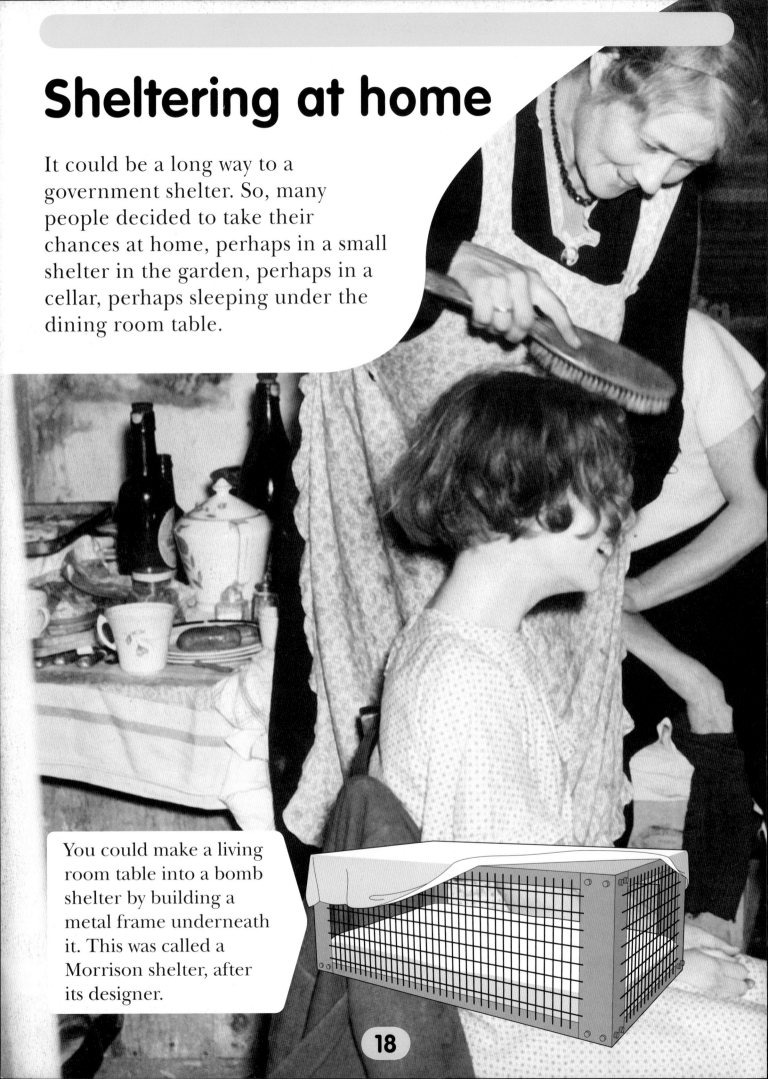

You could make a living room table into a bomb shelter by building a metal frame underneath it. This was called a Morrison shelter, after its designer.

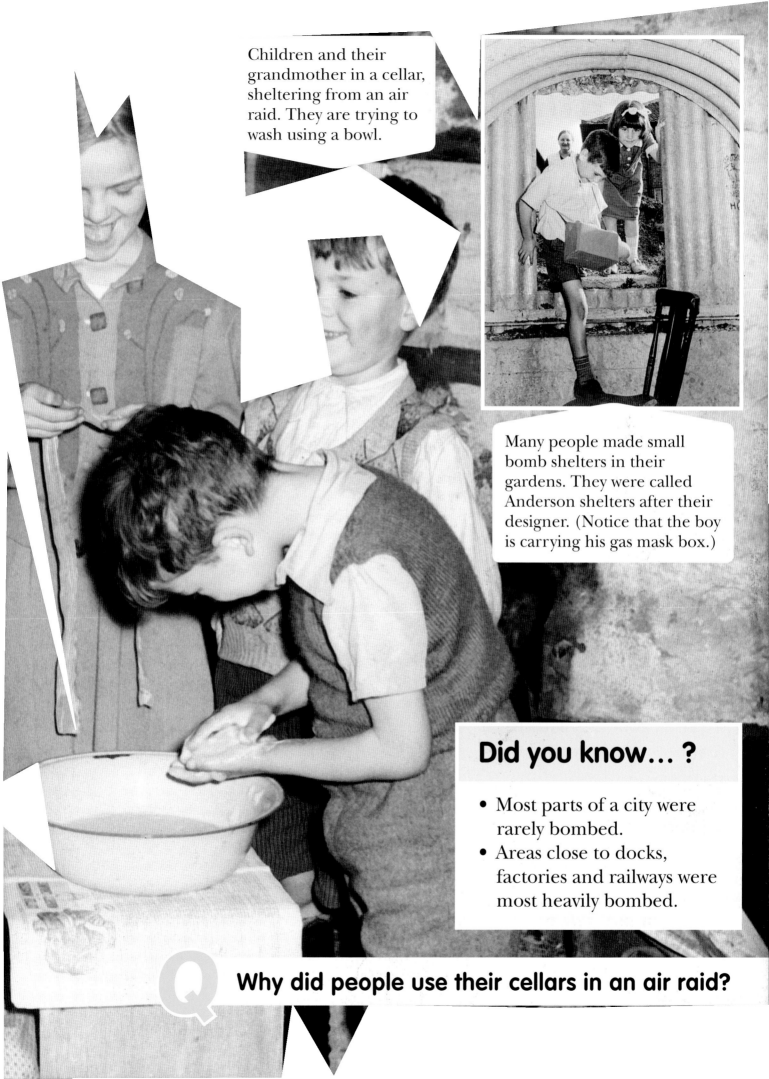

Children and their grandmother in a cellar, sheltering from an air raid. They are trying to wash using a bowl.

Many people made small bomb shelters in their gardens. They were called Anderson shelters after their designer. (Notice that the boy is carrying his gas mask box.)

Did you know... ?

- Most parts of a city were rarely bombed.
- Areas close to docks, factories and railways were most heavily bombed.

Q **Why did people use their cellars in an air raid?**

Evacuation

The government believed that there might be millions of deaths from bombing. In the first few days of the war they began to move a million children and their teachers from places near docks and railways where they might get bombed, to the safety of towns and villages in the countryside. This movement was called evacuation and it was known as "Operation Pied Piper".

Most children were not told exactly what was going to happen. Quite often they were simply told they were going on holiday with their school for a few days.

From the school they walked in 'crocodiles' or went in coaches with their teachers to the railway station, and from there to towns in the countryside. Some thought it was all noisy and confusing, while others thought it was an exciting adventure.

There was a danger that very young children might go astray or get lost. So each child was treated like a piece of luggage. Each one carried a gas mask, food and change of clothing and wore three labels saying who they were, where they had come from, and where they were going to. Then they were told, "Don't suck or eat your labels!".

Did you know… ?

- The government arranged for children to be sent to the USA, Canada and Australia. However, one of the evacuation ships was sunk by a German **torpedo** and 73 children were killed, so the overseas evacuation stopped.
- Evacuation did not involve children who lived in the outer parts of cities where bombs rarely fell.

Q What were the labels for?

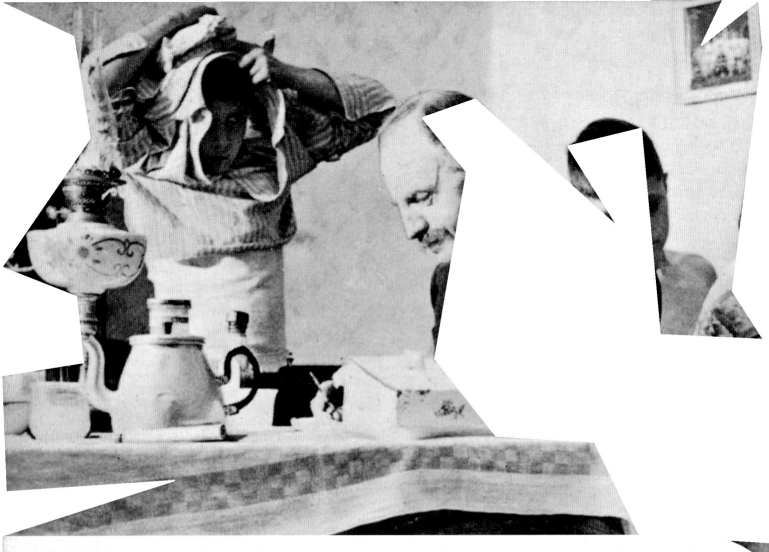

Being an evacuee

It was difficult trying to find new homes for such enormous numbers of children.

All of the spare rooms in every house in countryside villages were counted. These were to be used as homes (called billets) for the evacuees.

No-one was allowed to refuse children: if you had spare rooms, you got evacuees, and you had no idea who they were and where they were coming from. It was all in the hands of a local official called a billeting officer.

In many cases things did not go to plan. When the children arrived at their village there were often not enough spaces for them.

In many cases billeting officers lined the children up and asked local people to take their pick. Many children heard, "I'll take that one" and then found themselves whisked off… to the unknown.

Homes were much simpler in the 1940s than they are today. When there were extra children in the house they often had to line up to have a bath in the kitchen.

Did you know... ?

- Most children came from the poorest parts of cities and found themselves in the homes of much wealthier people.
- For some children it was their second evacuation. Jewish **refugees** from Hitler's Germany had only just arrived in Britain when they were evacuated to the country. Many did not speak a word of English.
- Many children became homesick and so went back to the cities to live with their mothers.

Q Why did children have to line up to bathe in the kitchen?

Dig for victory!

Britain is a small country with many people. It must get some of the food it needs from overseas.

The Germans believed they could beat the British by stopping these vital supplies arriving. They sent out their navy and submarines (U-boats) to sink ships carrying supplies to Britain across the Atlantic Ocean.

The Royal Navy tried to protect the ships. The struggle between the German and British navies was called the Battle of the Atlantic.

Because there was a risk that food might not get through, the government shared out the goods that were available through a system called rationing.

They also asked people to dig up any spare ground, such as gardens and even bomb sites, and grow extra vegetables.

Many children volunteered to help dig up extra land. This was called 'Dig for Victory'. Here they are digging a garden where a house once stood.

Oranges for children only: part of the rationing.

Did you know… ?

- Much of the wheat in British bread came from North America.
- Much cheese and butter came from Australia and New Zealand.
- Much of the tea came from India and Ceylon (now Sri Lanka).
- Much of the sugar came from the Caribbean.
- Petrol mostly came from the Middle East.
- Rubber for car tyres came from Malaya (now Malaysia).
- The Battle of the Atlantic was the longest military campaign of the Second World War, running from 1939 to 1945.

Q **Where could you grow extra vegetables near your home?**

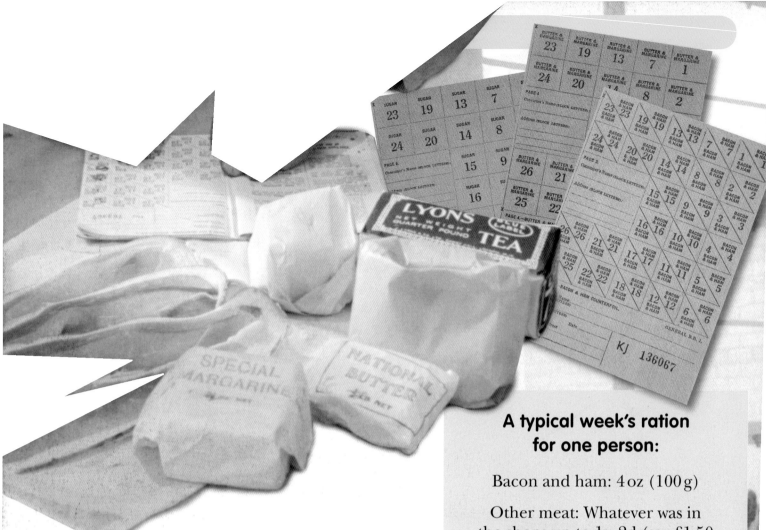

Weekly wartime food rations

It was important to know how much food a person needed to stay healthy. This was used to work out what the rations should be.

Some foods, such as potatoes, were all home grown and so were not rationed. Only foods in short supply were rationed. So the ration was not the whole amount of food people ate. What they did was to eat more potatoes and vegetables than we might today. Potatoes and carrots are healthy foods.

A typical week's ration for one person:

Bacon and ham: 4 oz (100 g)

Other meat: Whatever was in the shops up to 1s. 2d (say £1.50 today). Perhaps a pork chop and four sausages. (Liver, kidneys, heart and tripe were not rationed.)

Cheese: 2 oz (50 g)

Margarine: 4 oz (100 g)

Butter: 2 oz (50 g)

Sugar: 8 oz (225 g)

Milk: full cream milk 3 pints (1,800 ml). There was also 1 packet of dried milk every four weeks.

Jam: 1 lb (450 g) every two months

Tea: 2 oz (50 g) (about 2 teaspoonsful a day)

Eggs: 1 fresh egg. 1 packet of dried eggs every four weeks.

Sweets: 12 oz (350 g) every four weeks.

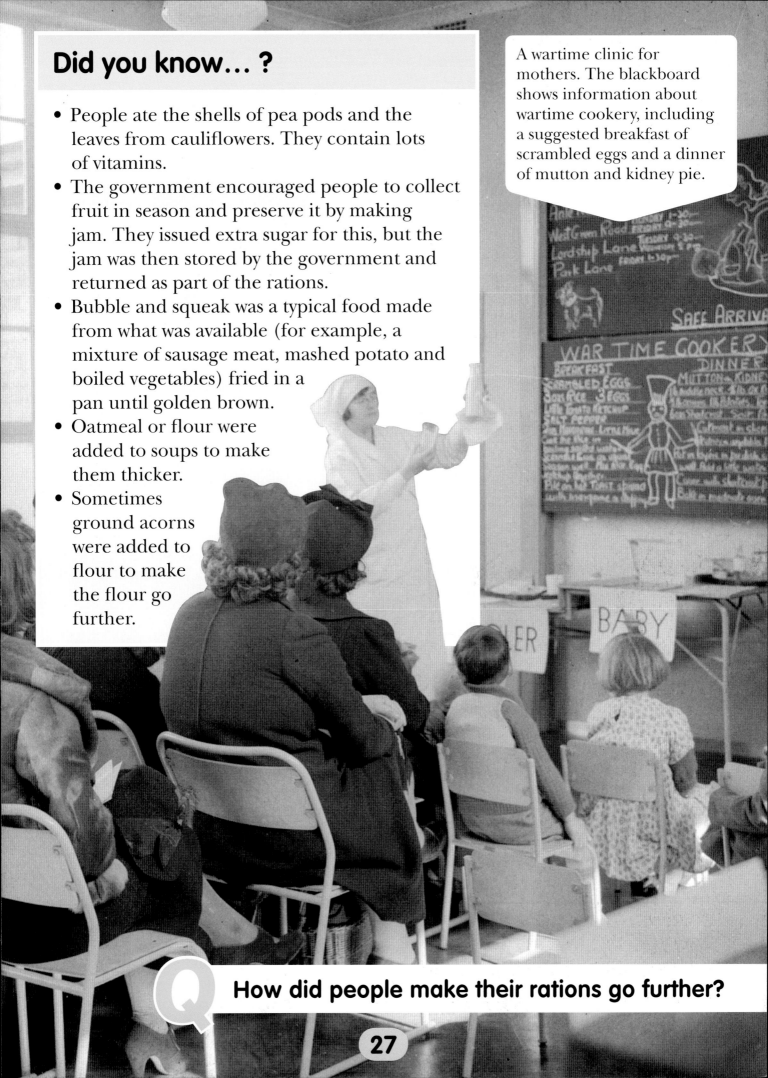

Did you know... ?

- People ate the shells of pea pods and the leaves from cauliflowers. They contain lots of vitamins.
- The government encouraged people to collect fruit in season and preserve it by making jam. They issued extra sugar for this, but the jam was then stored by the government and returned as part of the rations.
- Bubble and squeak was a typical food made from what was available (for example, a mixture of sausage meat, mashed potato and boiled vegetables) fried in a pan until golden brown.
- Oatmeal or flour were added to soups to make them thicker.
- Sometimes ground acorns were added to flour to make the flour go further.

A wartime clinic for mothers. The blackboard shows information about wartime cookery, including a suggested breakfast of scrambled eggs and a dinner of mutton and kidney pie.

How did people make their rations go further?

Wartime Christmas

People were too busy to have summer holidays, and most hotels were closed. So people made the most of Christmas.

With some of the family fighting overseas, it could not be an ordinary Christmas. Many children were also evacuees and were living away from home.

The government tried to help in small ways. For example, in the week before Christmas, they increased the tea and sugar rations.

People became very inventive about Christmas presents. Mums and dads might give each other a steel helmet or a leather gas mask case, some seeds and fertiliser (for growing vegetables at home). Or they might give the *Brighter Blackout Book*, which was full of suggested games during a blackout. Children got a bag of sweets. Parents got bars of soap. Although it was a hard time, everyone was determined to enjoy themselves.

Did you know... ?

- You could not have a beach holiday in summer because the beaches were covered in barbed wire to stop invasion.
- The blackout meant there were no lights in the shops or on outside Christmas trees.
- Rationing meant that it was hard to make a good Christmas meal.

Asleep at Christmas in an Anderson shelter.

At Christmas parties children dressed as nurses or air-raid wardens. Notice they got cups of tea to drink!

Q What Christmas present could you make without buying anything from the shops?

Try these...

Wartime radio broadcast

- Take a large sheet of cardboard (about 3 ft x 2 ft) and colour it black. Make a hole about 1 ft across and stick black fabric behind it. This is the speaker – all old radios had big speaker holes. Paint two knobs on the front – these are tuning and volume controls.

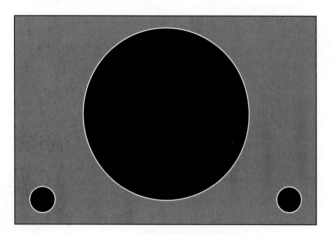

- Then turn down the lights. The teacher reads out the parts of the wartime speeches on pages 2, 11 and 13.
- Everyone in the class says how they might have felt if they had heard these speeches in the war.
- Now other members of the class make up plays, comedy shows or tell other listeners what it was like to be in the war. Each person sits behind the speaker, while the audience sits in front.

Christmas decoration

- You will need some colour scrap book paper (or crepe paper if you prefer).
- Cut some long thin strips, about 4 cm wide.
- Take two different coloured strips (eg. pink and yellow), and place one (pink) on top of the other (yellow) at right angles. Tape them together.
- Fold the bottom (yellow) strip up and across the top (pink) strip. Then fold the new bottom (pink) strip up and across the top (yellow).
- Keep plaiting the strips together until all the paper is used up. Tape them together and then pull the paper chain open carefully. Make as many as you like and tape them together.

Make animal powder (or body) puff gifts

In wartime people had to make their own toys. For these you need some felt, powder puffs* (or body puffs), cardboard and some pipe cleaners.

- Cut a panda shape from cardboard. Make the body the same size as the powder (or body) puff. Cover the cardboard with black felt. Stick the powder puff to the felt (or just slip the body puff loop over the panda's head). Stick white felt on for the face and eyes, and black for the nose, mouth and eye patches. Make the chick in the same way, but add some yellow pipe cleaner legs.

*Lamb's wool powder puffs were used for applying make-up during the Second World War, but are less common today. Our examples use the more readily available body puffs instead, and make a novel way of giving a body puff as a gift.

Swastika card game

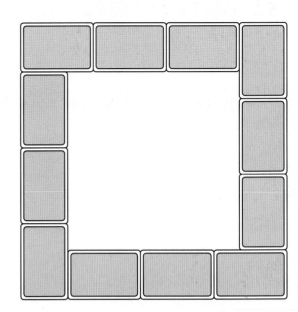

Make up a square with cards as shown here. Now take four more cards and make a German Nazi party swastika 卐 inside the card frame. (Hint: The cards themselves don't have to make up the swastika.)

Glossary

Ambassador A person representing the government in an overseas country.

blackout The government instruction that no light should show at night. All street lights were disconnected, car headlamps had special hoods and thick curtains had to be pulled across all windows.

concentration camp A kind of open prison. A place where people are herded together and kept in poor surroundings and often ill-treated.

conquer To take over a country by force.

darn, darned To mend with a criss-cross pattern of threads.

democracy A way in which people vote for a government and so have a say in what the country does. The UK and the USA are examples of democracies.

invade, invasion A movement of troops from one country to another with the intention of taking that country over by force.

Neutral countries Countries that did not take part in the war.

ration, rationing, rationed A system of giving out an equal amount of scarce items to everyone.

refugees People escaping the threat of death in their own country.

siren A device for making a very loud wailing sound of alarm.

torpedo A bomb in a long tube that could be fired underwater by a submarine. Torpedos had electric motors to move them through the water.

Index

(Curriculum Visions)

Curriculum Visions Explorers
This series provides straightforward introductions to key worlds and ideas.

You might also be interested in
Our slightly more detailed book, 'Children in the Second World War'. There is a Teacher's Guide to match 'Children in the Second World War'. Additional notes in PDF format are also available from the publisher to support 'Exploring the Second World War'. All of these products are suitable for KS2.

Dedicated Web Site
Watch movies, see many more pictures and read much more in detail about children in the Second World War:

www.curriculumvisions.com
(Professional Zone: subscription required)

A CVP Book
Copyright © 2007 Earthscape

First reprint 2008

The right of Brian Knapp to be identified as the author of this work has been asserted by him in accordance with the Copyright, Designs and Patents Act 1988.

All rights reserved. No part of this publication may be reproduced, stored in a retrieval system, or transmitted in any form or by any means, electronic, mechanical, photocopying, recording or otherwise, without prior permission of the copyright holder.

Author
Brian Knapp, BSc, PhD

Educational Consultants
JM Smith (former Deputy Head of Wellfield School, Burnley, Lancashire); the Librarians of Hertfordshire School Library Service

Senior Designer
Adele Humphries, BA

Editor
Gillian Gatehouse

Photographs
The Earthscape Picture Library, except *Corbis* p6–7, 12–13, 14–15, 16–17 (main), 18–19 (main), 20–21, 28–29; *The Illustrated London News* p22–23; *The Imperial War Museum* p4–5 (D3173), 10–11(MH6547), 19 (inset)(D778), 24–25 (D8957), 26–27 (D467); *ShutterStock* p8–9, 11 (inset).

Illustrations
David Woodroffe

Designed and produced by
Earthscape

Printed in China by
WKT Company Ltd

Exploring the Second World War – Curriculum Visions
A CIP record for this book is available from the British Library
ISBN 978 1 86214 206 0

This product is manufactured from sustainable managed forests. For every tree cut down at least one more is planted.